THE
ACOUSTIC GUITAR
REPAIR
DETECTIVE

Case Studies of Steel-String Guitar Diagnoses and Repairs

Also Nylon-String Guitars and Ukuleles!

By Paul Neri

Illustrations by Scott Baldwin

ISBN 978-1-4950-6915-4

7777 W. BLUEMOUND RD. P.O. BOX 13819 MILWAUKEE, WI 53213

In Australia Contact:
Hal Leonard Australia Pty. Ltd.
4 Lentara Court
Cheltenham, Victoria, 3192 Australia
Email: ausadmin@halleonard.com.au

Visit Hal Leonard Online at
www.halleonard.com

About the Author

Paul Neri has been repairing and restoring fretted instruments since 1980 and runs Neri Lutherie in his home in Clinton, Connecticut.

He has performed as a solo guitarist and in various jazz, bluegrass and duos on drums, banjo and guitar respectively. "Performing has always guided me in understanding the subtleties and importance of a professional set up on any string instrument," he said.

I would like to thank:

George Youngblood for teaching me the fine art of repair and starting my career where there once was none; Scott Baldwin for his beautiful illustrations, along with continual help in design, editing, and artistic direction; Peter Neri for his masterful editing; my wife, Eileen O'Donnell, for her unending support and additional illustrations; my musical parents, brothers, and sister; Joe Tinari, for his inspirational guitar instruction and support through my guitar repair journey; Tom Bazzolo, for his support and collegial conversation on the fine points of guitar building; Hugh, Liam, and Nola for giving me the reason and drive to finish this little book; all my loyal and word-of-mouth customers who keep me in business, especially the sensitive and demanding clients (you know who you are), because you push me to discover new techniques and open my mind to new possibilities as it relates to setting up your guitars with better accuracy; and The Martin Guitar company for using me as a representative to repair their instruments.

Introduction v
Humidity 1
    Case 1 3
    Case 2 4
    Case 3 6
    Case 4 7
    Case 5 8
Cracks (Loss of Humidity) 10
    Case 6 12
Braces 14
    Case 7 15
Bridge Plates 17
    Case 8 19
Frets 21
    Case 9 22
Assessing Guitar Action with a
Trio of Adjustments 24
    Truss Rod 25
    Case 10 25
    Case 11 27
    Nut 27
    Case 12 27
    Saddle 29
    Case 13 29
    Case 14 30
    Case 15 31
Intonation 33
    Case 16 34
    Case 17 35
Neck Angle 36
    Case 18 38

More Facts 40
   Tuning Machines 41
      Case 19 41
   Strings and String Changing 43
      Case 20 43
      Case 21 45
      Case 22 46
   Strap Buttons 46
   End Pins 47
      Case 23 47
   Buying a Used Guitar 48
      Case 24 48
   Cleaning and Polishing 50
      Case 25 50
   The 12-string Guitar 51
      Case 26 51
   Case 27 51
   Ukuleles 52
      Case 28 52
   Archtop Guitars 52
      Case 29 53
   The Classical Guitar 55
   The Hybrid Nylon-string Guitar 57
   The Flamenco Guitar 57
   The Case for Cases 58
   Pickups 59
Odds and Ends 61
   Test Review 64
   Answers 65
Troubleshooting 66
Glossary 74

Introduction

This book was written to help any acoustic guitar player diagnose common problems relating to the adjustment, upkeep, and repair of his/her guitar. While reading, you will also learn common guitar terminology.

I am also keen on making you understand the reasons why guitars go through changes that need your attention. I estimate that I have repaired 15,000 guitars in my 35+ years of repairing all styles of guitars, so I have some experience in what I have noted here. My aim is not to encourage do-it-yourself repair, but to understand everything about a guitar as it relates to playability, with an eye on preventing common guitar problems. A number of "cases" are outlined throughout the text; some are common questions, but most are myths perpetuated by guitarists.

Playability is the real thrust behind these writings. The string action, or how easily the guitar plays, isn't always determined by just what you see at the fretboard (i.e., making saddle, truss rod, and nut adjustments). Also keep an eye on the structure of the instrument and how it ultimately relates to the action.

To go a little more in depth and help familiarize yourself with common action measurements, I recommend buying a 6-inch ruler in 1/64-inch increments (you can usually find this in a hardware store as a machinist's rule) and a 24-inch ruler or straightedge for measuring top and back straightness and neck angle. Any references to measurements as it pertains to action are not hard and fast; there are always exceptions to these measurements, so they are only meant as a general guide.

Before I write about setting action, attention must be paid to the stability of the guitar body, especially the top, where an average of 165 pounds of pressure is constantly pulling and tugging at its integrity.

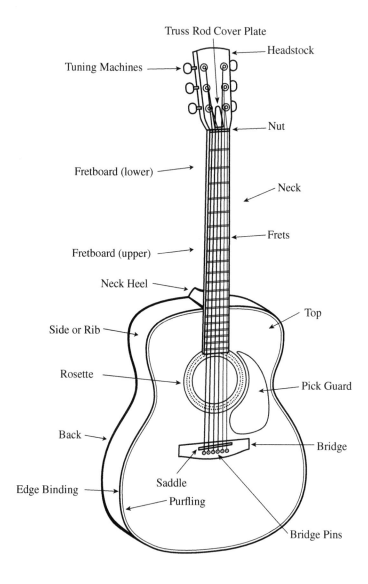

Truss Rod Cover Plate

Headstock

Tuning Machines

Nut

Fretboard (lower)

Neck

Frets

Fretboard (upper)

Neck Heel

Top

Side or Rib

Rosette

Pick Guard

Back

Bridge

Edge Binding

Saddle

Purfling

Bridge Pins

HUMIDITY

Your Guitar's Best Friend
(In the Dry Winter Months)

Humidity, especially the lack of it, is the most singular cause of both action shift and structural degradation.

Modern, hotter, and drier houses in colder climates with better insulation contribute to guitars cracking prematurely. *For this reason every precaution must be taken to humidify guitars during the dry season.*

The most important thing you can do is to *keep your guitar in a hardshell case when not in use* (I know it isn't popular with those of you who love looking at your guitar on a stand or wall). I routinely see the most shrinkage and cracks in guitars that are mostly kept out of their cases.

Owning a guitar humidifier is also a must. The most popular types are:

- The hose and sponge (Dampit and Humitron)
- The rubber and sponge soundhole cover (Kyser Lifeguard)
- The hard plastic and sponge fit-between-strings (Planet Waves GH)
- The disposable, all-year-round humidifying and dehumidifying, no water (Planet Waves Humidipak)
- The permeable tube and crystal water absorbent (Oasis)

Homemade humidifiers are also acceptable. A plastic soap dish with a series of 1/8" holes drilled into the top is an example. A humidifier is only as good as the care you give it:

- keep the sponge or humidifying element moist at all times;
- keep the guitar in the case when not in use; and
- keep the case closed at all times. Think of the guitar case as a micro environment.

CASE 1:

"Why is the finish on the bottom of my guitar, at the end pin, coming off?"

Any sponge type of humidifier has the potential to drip if you don't wring it out and dry the outside of the hose thoroughly. This type of humidifier doesn't hold much moisture and hardens with age, causing it to hold less water and drip more. Loosening of the finish and surrounding water stains are good indications that the guitar was stored on an instrument stand, with the finish damage being caused from a dripping humidifier that wasn't wrung out properly.

The Humidipak is one choice for storage when you can't keep up with water refilling. It is a set of three sealed packs in mesh bags that both suspend in the sound hole and fit in the guitar case. Although they are effective in controlling both excessive humidity and dryness, they don't last long in harsh environments and are the most expensive.

I like the Oasis because it holds a good amount of water, is reasonably priced, is non-marring, compact, does not drip, and shrivels up as an indicator that it needs refilling.

All concerns about controlling humidity are useless without knowing the level of relative humidity (R.H.) in your home. For this reason, owning some sort of digital hygrometer (humidity-reading instrument) is a must. Small hygrometers are sold at smoke shops, as they are used to monitor cigar and pipe-tobacco moisture. They cost about $20.00. Their small size is ideal for keeping them in a guitar case. For more money, Planet Waves has a hygrometer unit that records the highs and lows of humidity over time. Martin Guitar and Oasis sell small rectangular-shaped ones. Larger table or wall-mounted ones are sold at Radio Shack. Using an analog or dial-type hygrometer is less accurate—unless you spend a lot of money for a professional one. The analog element that senses humidity needs to be periodically recalibrated with a sling psychrometer and recharged; otherwise, the sensor will harden, giving you a false, non-fluctuating reading regardless of the actual relative humidity. Cheap hygrometers ($10.00 and under) found on the internet cannot be trusted.

CASE 2:

"I love looking at my guitar on the stand. I'm more apt to play it when I don't keep it in the case.
I don't understand why the action gets so out of
whack in the winter. I think the guitar is defective."

Ideally, dry-season humidity levels should be in the 40-50% range. Super cold and dry outside temperatures and very warm and dry inside temperatures (70+ degrees) make it almost impossible to maintain any kind of moderate guitar-friendly climate. You can compound problems related to shrinking and cracking of guitar wood by leaving the guitar on a stand or out of the case. When household wooden chairs loosen, wooden doors close easier, and steam from a shower disappears quickly from the bathroom mirror, your house is well below 40%. In fact, by the peak of the dry season, you may see humidity readings near 15 to 20% r.h. if no actions are taken.

To assess shrinkage of the guitar top or back, use a 24" straightedge. To assess the top, lay the straightedge across the top from the lower bout bass side, just behind the bridge, to the lower bout treble side. The straight edge should rock on the center rise, with a deflection no greater than 1/4" if the straightedge is held firm to either binding edge. Most guitars are built with a gentle arch. Severe shrinkage causes the guitar top and top braces to shrink so much that there is space below the straightedge along its entire length. Lesser degrees of shrinkage enable the straightedge to touch the area behind the bridge but show air space between the binding edge and the center of the bridge area. Distortions between the bridge and soundhole area signify a shrinkage problem (see illustration).

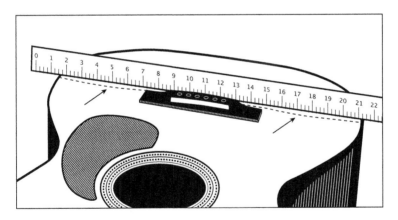

Top shrinkage from over-dried top

Examine the back curvature to assess degrees of shrinkage. A perfectly hydrated guitar back has an evenly rounded arch from the center to both edges of both bouts. The back is generally more arched than the top so it is easier to see the effects of shrinkage. Severe shrinkage dries out the braces and back to the point that a straightedge laid across the back will touch the outer binding, with air space in the middle.

Some of my clients have whole-house humidifiers as part of their heating systems. Even though this helps, it offers a false sense of security, which leads to leaving the guitar out of its case. The humidifier only works when the furnace is running, which leaves a lot of downtime. Keeping the guitar in a humidified case is still needed because I've seen guitars crack when a humidified furnace system was used without also using a guitar humidifier.

Guitars assembled with unseasoned wood, or in humid climates where no humidity control is exercised, shrink when brought into a drier climate. The neck is especially affected by changes in humidity. Usually, excess humidity will back-bow a neck causing a rise in the center of the fingerboard. The effect is buzzing in the first four frets. Excess humidity will bulge the area behind the bridge causing it to rise. However, the rise in string height at the bridge creates an uncomfortable combination of uneven action. The best thing to do is to have the guitar adjusted for summer or humid-season playability, possibly with a lower saddle, retaining the taller saddle for winter or drier-season play. Wider-bodied jumbo guitars like the Martin J-40, Gibson J-200 and the Guild F-50 and F-212 fluctuate in swelling and shrinking the most in their winter-to-summer swings.

CASE 3:

"I live in a damp area by the coast. I keep the guitar
in the case when not being played, but the action is high,
the finish is blushed white, and the top is bulging a lot.
I can't control the humidity. What can I do?"

Evidence of excess humidity can be seen as a blush under the surface of the finish. I've seen this occur when a guitar case is left in a non-dehumidified basement in the summer or in a very moist case. You can use a hair dryer to reduce the moisture buildup in the guitar case. Simply open the empty case and blow-dry the interior for 15 minutes. Check the R.H. with a hygrometer by leaving it in the case for 15 minutes prior to blow-drying and after blow-drying to see if you have lowered the humidity level to about 45%. You might have to do this routine once or twice a week if the room that it is in is very humid and you leave the case open for long periods of time.

CASE 4:

"I think the guy who did the last fret job screwed up.
Look at how far the frets are sticking out!"

It's possible that the fret replacement was done in the humid summer months, when the fretboard is at its most swollen. Lack of adequate humidity affects guitar necks as much as tops, backs, and sides. Sometimes it is the first place on the guitar that will show the affects of shrinkage: with string tension released, tuning machine screw-down bushings show looseness as the peg head loses dimension. Fretboards shrink laterally, giving the effect that frets are growing. When this happens, frets need to be edge-filed flush to the edge of the fretboard. If the fretboard is bound in plastic, excessive dryness can creates wavy separations and may even cause binding splits at the fret junctures (see illustration). Ebony, although hard and durable and the best choice for

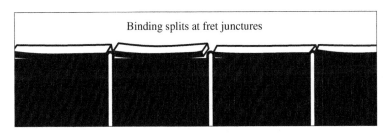
Binding splits at fret junctures

fretboards, is unstable and easily cracked if moderate humidity levels are not maintained. Unlike tops that crack, cracks in fretboards made of ebony or rosewood are easily filled and concealed with glue and matching wood dust. The worst part about shrinking fretboards is the possibility that it can pull cracks in the top, adjoining the upper fretboard edge. Classical guitars are particularly susceptible to this because their fretboards have a greater thickness and mass. When cracks occur in steel-string tops, the possibility of top failure increases because of the greater string tension that exerts a collapsing pressure. Necks pull in, braces let go, neck blocks pull forward, dimpling the sides, and soundholes distort when the fretboard extension pulls forward. Dryness also can peel the fretboard extension off the top, creating a similar condition that was just outlined, as the neck has freedom to move toward the soundhole (see illustration on the next page).

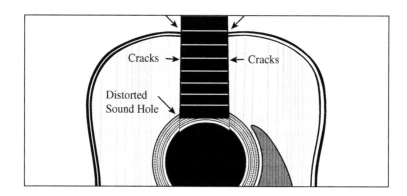

Cracks → | ← Cracks

Distorted
Sound Hole

CASE 5:

"I just went into the restaurant for an hour.
You're telling me I can't leave the guitar in the trunk?"

Temperatures in a car trunk on a hot summer day can reach the limit of the glue's ability to hold the guitar's bridge in place.

Bridges occasionally need to be re-glued because of overexposure to heat, excess humidity, or glue failure due to bad clamping pressure or inadequate wood-to-wood bonding. Bridges are glued to the top usually with yellow aliphatic wood glue. 160-180 pounds (240 pounds for a 12-string) of string tension is constantly tugging at the bridge and guitar top, so any overheating or top deflection will help to loosen the bond. Even though the bridge may still be mostly attached, it can actually slip forward, re-attaching itself when cooled, raking the lacquer in a wave pattern in front of the bridge. Even a guitar left on an instrument stand in direct sunlight or next to a wood stove can begin lifting the back end of the bridge.

Excessive humidity will swell the guitar top, rejecting the bridge, and start the process of de-lamination of the bridge-to-top join. Excessive dryness also causes the bridge to become unglued. For cosmetic reasons, some guitars are manufactured with a generous outline of lacquer around the inside perimeter of the bridge footprint. The result is what appears to be a lifting bridge, when, in reality, it is only about 1/8" of separation due to the inability of wood glue to adhere to lacquer. This apparent separation may never worsen, but if other environmental conditions exist, it may begin detaching over time. It is always best to err on the side of caution and only re-glue a bridge if it is truly coming off. Every time a bridge is re-glued, no matter how careful one is in removing it, some wood loss from the guitar top is inevitable (see illustration).

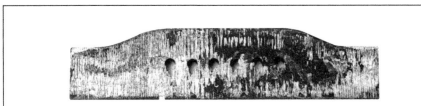

Even using heat to soften the glue, some wood fiber
is still attached to the bridge after removal

To check how far a bridge is lifting, slip a piece of paper in the opening. If it can be inserted along the entire length of the bridge and is deeper than 1/8", a luthier should be consulted for a possible removal and re-gluing. Merely "shoving" glue in the separation rarely holds because you are still faced with trying to glue wood to lacquer. Old glue from the original bond acts as a barrier to new glue and wood glue does not work as a gap-filler (see illustration).

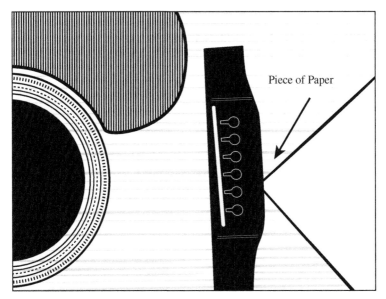

Piece of Paper

If paper is able to enter under the entire length of bridge more that 1/8",
consult a luthier for a possible re-gluing

CRACKS
(Loss of Humidity)

No one likes them,
especially repair people

Loss of humidity is more critical to the guitar's structural integrity than excess (60-75%) humidity. Dryness causes sagging and warping of the top, leading to cracking. Plywood or laminated-wood guitars are subject to veneer cracks, but rarely do they split through.

Determine which parts of your guitar are solid wood, and which are laminates. To see if you have a solid-top guitar, look down the edge of the soundhole and follow the growth-ring lines (grain). A solid top's lines will continue all the way through, whereas a laminate top will have a non-distinct, horizontal three-layered look (see illustration).

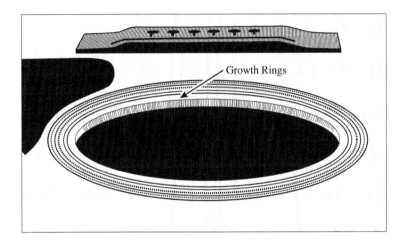

High-quality guitar woods are cut to gain the most in strength and tone. The top wood, usually spruce or cedar, is cut so that the grain lines you see run perpendicular to the plane of the top (called "quarter sawn"). This grain alignment gives strength to oppose the constant pull of string tension, enhancing string vibration. The tonally alive guitar top is thinly dimensioned to make the best use of the wood's inherent strength. The only drawback is that it is more prone to cracking along its growth-ring lines. If you have ever split firewood kindling you know that it takes little effort to split wood if your axe follows the direction of the grain (growth-ring lines). Lateral pulling forces across the top increase with dryness. Given just enough dryness, the top wood is poised to crack at any given moment. Sides and backs are also subject to the same splitting forces, though not as much as the top. The top is under direct string tension and its makeup of softer, more fragile wood makes it more prone to cracking than the sides or back.

Here, a mandolin top is showing severe finish "crazing," or "checking"

Excessive dryness, humidity, or temperature change can cause cracks, or "crazes," to an instrument's finish. The type of effect depends on the type of finish: a crackled pottery-glaze look (cracks), or long striations following the wood grain lines (crazes–see illustration). It's easy to tell if the crack is only in the finish if it veers off of parallel from the grain lines, although it can originate from a crack.

CASE 6:

"You fixed this crack last fall. How come it opened up?
I lost the humidifier you sold me, but I didn't think I needed
it because you had already hydrated the guitar last year."

Dry-season cracks are a concern every year. Old guitars that have survived countless years with no cracks can still crack if the humidity is low enough for an extended period of time. If a crack forms in the top, it should be glued soon after it forms. It usually means the entire guitar is too dry. When I repair this type of crack, I first take an internal R.H. reading and judge how much of the cracking is due to an over-dry top or the occasional weak grain line. I then rehydrate the guitar with a series of moist sponges, with the soundhole covered in its case – monitoring it over the course of three-to-five days. As soon as humidity is stabilized and the crack is closed enough for its edges to touch, but open enough to move up and down, I'll glue and reinforce it.

Older cracks in guitars that have lost their ability to rehydrate to original specs need a matching splint of wood glued into the open crack. This is the least desirable type of repair both for cosmetics and for its high cost. For these reasons, all efforts to keep the guitar as close to 50% R.H., especially in the heating season, is necessary. Once R.H. levels reach 40% you are entering the danger zone. When you get below 40% and there's a decrease in string action, fret "sprouting" (when frets protrude out of each side of the fretboard) may occur and possible cracks may form.

For any repaired crack to hold, proper humidity levels must be maintained in the dry months. Otherwise, more cracks or the reopening of original cracks are inevitable.

BRACES

Top braces control tone and structure and **back braces** affect structure and sound projection

CASE 7:

"I hear a buzz. I think the top braces are loose."

An internal inspection of a guitar is a must when determining its overall structural integrity.

Under non-accidental circumstances, braces can come loose in specific areas. The first place to check for loose braces is in the back. When loose, these braces affect tone more than most top-brace detachment. The back serves as a reflective plate. If dampened by loose braces, the general tone and projection is affected. To diagnose, simply rap your knuckle, all around the back, especially at brace-end areas. Listen for a clear tone. Any dull or "cracked dish" sound denotes looseness.

With a hypodermic syringe filled with glue, a luthier can repair a loose brace by injecting glue between a loose or fractured brace and back, using brace jacks to clamp. If glue is merely injected without good internal clamping, a deformation of the back will occur.

Typical top-brace detachments are located at the X-brace area under the bridge wings and at the soundhole area on the forward ends of the X-brace. The reason these areas are especially vulnerable is due to the pull of the strings that rotates the bridge down in front and up in back. A neck angle that is too steep worsens the condition, as the leverage increases the tilting action of the bridge top.

In addition to a poorly glued brace, environmental conditions play a role in top distortion. If swollen from humidity, the top expands and "over-domes." This condition helps to release the bridge wings as they struggle to remain straight and stay attached. Once the bridge wings come unglued, the bridge continues to rotate and lever down, causing:

- braces to detach underneath the bridge;
- the bridge plate to warp; and
- the soundhole area to cave in, further releasing the X-brace ends beside the soundhole.

Oftentimes, you can see from the outside, what is happening on the inside. Doming, or top-arching, is normal for most flat-top guitars, but an uneven arching characterized by a sharply defined bump just behind the bridge wing indicates the X-brace is loose alongside the bridge plate (see illustration).

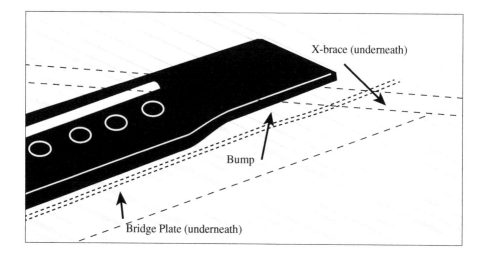

X-brace (underneath)

Bump

Bridge Plate (underneath)

BRIDGE PLATES

hat you don't see can have a
rge effect on structure

The bridge plate is glued to the top, inside the X-brace cross over under the bridge. It is made from hardwood, usually maple or rosewood, and serves the dual function of both securing the string ball ends against the bridge pins and maintaining top stability in this high-stress area. Even expensive or "boutique" guitars may show bridge-plate distortion over time. This is caused by environmental extremes, long periods of storage under full string tension, or use of heavier gauged strings than the guitar was built for. Distortion in the bridge-plate area is worsened by a neck angle that is too steep. The result is a bridge and saddle set too high for playable action, which exhibits more forward pull, causing detached bridges and over-stressed and bulging tops (see illustration).

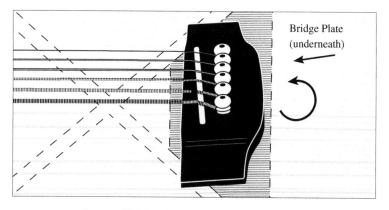

A warped bridge plate and forward-leaning bridge

Inexpensive guitars usually have unsuitable wood, like spruce plywood, as bridge-plate material. This is possibly the worst choice, as it is soft and pliable and easily crushed and warped by the full pressure exerted by the string ball ends. In a short time, the ball ends crush through the bridge plate, causing top damage and increasing chances of pulling the bridge off. Another problem is that string windings appear as the ball end crushes through the top. The intonation, string height and tone all are affected by the thick windings coming to bear on the bridge saddle. The inflexible windings and different thicknesses create uneven string heights and decreased string-to-saddle contact. The end result is sustain loss and intonation problems.

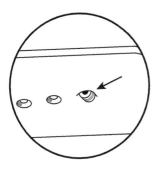

Worn Bridge-Plate Hole

String windings exposed from worn bridge plate and short saddle

Bridge-plate replacement is in order if it is both warped and worn. If the bridge plate is large, mostly intact, and well-adhered, I prefer to leave it attached and steam-press it flat. If it is worn out in the string-hole area, I attach a small (5/8" x 3" x 1/8") hardwood bridge-plate overlay which offers a new surface for the ball ends to sit against.

CASE 8:

"My friend said that if I change my bridge pins to brass, I will hear a dramatic difference in sustain."

Worn-out plastic bridge pins create an environment that quickens bridge-plate string-hole wear. Replace bridge pins when they bend or splay. This worn-out condition makes it easier for the strings' ball ends to crush up into the bridge plate (see illustration of deformed bridge pin). Harder bridge-pin materials help to extend bridge-plate life but contribute little to tone (although I know many guitarists who would disagree).

Originally, all bridge pins were made of wood, hard plastic, or bone and had no flutes to guide the string. The bridge plates and bridges then had to be sawn to allow the string to nestle between the pin and plate. This is a much better way of joining the string to the bridge plate as it makes the string ball end come to rest totally on the bridge-plate surface.

The current, typical soft, fluted plastic bridge pin allows the string ball end to crush against it, deforming it while driving it into the string hole. This results in premature wear of the bridge plate and a higher probability that the bridge will become detached from the ball ends reaching through to the top and into the bridge bottom. Guitars can be modified by using the older solid-bridge pin method just described (see illustration).

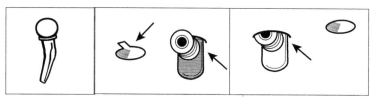

| Deformed Bridge Pin | Sawn string notch keeps ball end on plate instead of in plate hole | Typical unsawn bridge plate |

The frets and the fretboard are some of the most important parts of the guitar as it relates to feel and playability. Dented, flattened, loose, and poorly sanded frets cause multiple problems, from poor intonation to poor sustain or dead notes.

CASE 9:

*"I can't keep my guitar in tune.
It's really getting hard to play, too."*

The level of the frets is only as good as the level of the fretboard. A luthier must assess whether an uneven fret level is due to fretboard warp, delamination, fret looseness, unevenness, or normal fret wear. Typical wear is caused by normal string depression and the technique of hammering strings onto the frets. String wear ranges from mild to severely V-notched. If play-ing technique involves bending strings, flat spots develop. These conditions result in uneven sustain, intonation problems, string buzz, and hard action because of the extra squeezing needed to depress the strings against the bottom of the string divots. Flattened fret tops feel sharp and squared-off, making the fretboard uncomfortable and slow (see illustration).

Before final action is set, the frets have to be trued so that low string height can be achieved without unnecessary string buzz. Fret leveling, or dressing, is a routine repair. The process involves leveling high, low, and worn fret areas and then re-crowning and polishing them. If five or more frets are so dented that more than half of their original height (.040") is worn, replacement is preferable to leveling them into the rest of the frets.

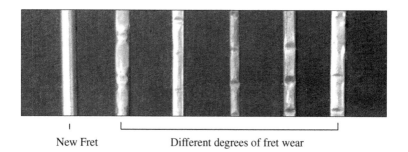

New Fret   Different degrees of fret wear

Complete fret replacement is an option when more than 12 frets are worn, when the majority of frets are loose, or for any other fretboard abnormality as deemed by a qualified luthier.

Common fret widths for acoustic guitars vary from .080" to .110." Martin and Taylor guitars use .080" while Gibson uses .090" to .100." Fret height is .040"-.045." Extra-high frets (.050") are also becoming more common in order to reduce the number of times needed to re-fret a guitar. Most companies install frets without the use of glue. Refretting an older fretboard sometimes requires the use of glue to help stabilize the fret slot and help hold down the frets.

Some feel that increased sustain and clearer tone are the benefits of changing to a new and slightly wider fret size. Some of the effect comes from a fret that fits tighter to a worn slot, making more solid contact with the neck. Merely having a new, undented fret is the chief reason for better tone. Fret wear happens gradually and you can easily become accustomed to a less-distinct tone. After fret replacement, the guitar returns to its original tone qualities.

ASSESSING GUITAR ACTION WITH A TRIO OF ADJUSTMENTS

The setup of any guitar requires these adjustments

After a structural diagnosis is noted, only then can a longer-lasting adjustment be made on the action. Check the trio of action adjustments in order, starting with:

- the truss rod
- the nut
- the saddle

TRUSS ROD
CASE 10:

"The action was high, so I tightened the truss rod to lower the action. Now it's buzzing but the action is still high. I made sure I loosened all the strings because I heard that you should never adjust the truss rod with the string tension on."

The truss rod is the "go-to" fix for the guitarist trying to change action. Unfortunately, it is the least understood part of the guitar and consequently is adjusted with no clear idea of what it is doing or how far to adjust it. A truss-rod adjustment on a well-functioning rod is always made with the string tension on. This is the only way to accurately assess what effect you are having as you turn the adjustment nut. The only exceptions are on guitars where the nut is hidden inside the soundhole, requiring the string tension to be loosened to fit a wrench on the truss-rod nut, or when the truss rod is as tight as it can go. In these cases, a further assessment is needed before any further action is taken.

Note: Some guitars have no adjustable truss rod, most notably Martin guitars before the year 1985. Non-adjustable truss rods can still be coaxed with fretboard heat warping if straightening or bowing is needed.

If the action is high (i.e., the string height looks or feels stiff), do the following while the guitar is in playing position (checking truss-rod adjustment in any other position—for example, lying flat on a table—could influence neck flex, thus influencing string height and neck bow): Depress or capo the strings at the first fret while depressing the 14th fret, or wherever the body join is located and look at the space between the bottom of the string and the top of the midway sixth or seventh fret. This distance should be no greater than .010".

Using a standard piece of computer paper or a thin business card as a feeler gauge for a general (not definitive) setting, you can measure this gap. I like to use both the low E string and the high E string heights as references because there can be varying degrees of disparity between the opposite sides of the neck. Different readings can signal a twist in the neck. This is a condition that a truss-rod adjustment cannot fix. In extreme cases, it leads to uneven action and needs attention by way of either heat warping or refretting to correct. A mild differential slightly favoring more bow to the bass side is acceptable and even desirable, for one whose playing style favors a strong attack on the bass strings, like a bluegrass player (see illustration).

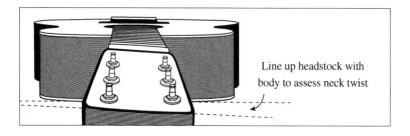

Line up headstock with body to assess neck twist

It is customary to adjust the truss rod with full string tension on as it does not harm the neck (see illustration).

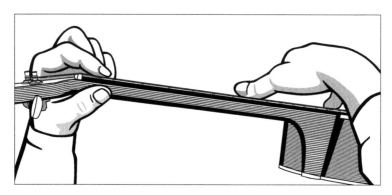

Tapping the string on the fretboard with the thumb to determine neck relief– .008-.010" gap at 6th-7th fret

If the neck is forward, or positive-bowed (neck pulled down, away from the strings), the truss rod must be tightened, usually in a clockwise direction. A back-bowed neck (strings too close to the fretboard) means the truss rod needs loosening. As a rule, if the first playing position notes (frets 1-4) are buzzing but buzzing decreases as you play up the neck, this is an indicator that the truss rod is too tight. If, after tightening the truss rod, the string height is too high and the bridge and saddle and nut are adjusted to their lowest points, the neck angle should be checked.

Note: Some truss rods tighten by a counter-clockwise motion, while others are "two-way" in that they can tighten or loosen a neck from a neutral position.

CASE 11:

*"You just adjusted the truss rod a
week ago and it's back-bowed again."*

Sometimes extreme weather can affect necks quickly; other times it could be a truss rod that is bound in the neck and continues to tighten over time until it is released from the bound-up condition.

NUT

CASE 12:

*"I wanted to raise the action because I was getting buzzes
at the ninth to 12th frets, so I put some paper in the nut
slots and I still have the buzzes and the action feels stiff."*

Once there is a reasonable adjustment to the neck, the nut-slot heights must be checked. This adjustment does ultimately affect the final string height at the saddle but shouldn't be used as a way to change the action. The nut adjustment affects the feel of the strings at the first fret positions. It should be adjusted as low as possible without producing open string buzz. *Remember: once the string is depressed on any fret, the nut is no longer part of either a buzz or a height adjustment further on down the fretboard.*

To check for slot depth, depress each string one at a time behind the second fret with your finger or depress all the strings at once with a capo. Look at the space between the bottom of the string and the top of the first fret. A rough measurement is about .010", or ten thousandths of an inch, use a thin business card as a feeler gauge (see illustration on next page). If the nut is very low, I tap the string just ahead of the nut to hear a pinging sound that signals that there is still some space between the fret and string. If there is no space between the first fret and the string–the string is literally laying on the first fret–then the nut must be shimmed from beneath with a hard, thin material, filled at the slot, or replaced. The only time the string will not buzz on the open string and the nut slot is cut too low is when either the truss rod is extremely bowed away from the strings or the action at the saddle is very high.

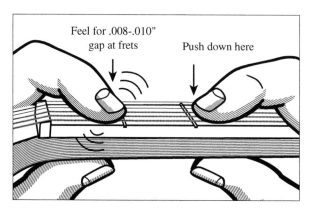

Checking string height at first fret by feeling
the space between the string and first fret

I prefer nut replacement only when either the nut is soft plastic, spacing of the strings is uneven, or when refretting. (Refretting generally raises the fret height compared to the worn-out ones, thereby making the old nut height too low.) Shimming the nut from underneath is an acceptable repair as long as it is a hard material and matches the nut color. Shimming the nut does not affect tone, but could affect stability if crudely made.

The choice of material, as in the choice of bridge-pin material, is inconsequential with respect to its affect on tone. The open string tone is affected by the nut when its slots are filed or angled incorrectly, causing a dampened effect.

Once the string is depressed, the nut is no longer part of the tone equation. Only soft plastic is a problem both because of its lack of smooth string movement and because of its tone absorption at the open string. Hard plastics like Micarta or Corian, "tusq," bone-bleached or unbleached, fossilized ivory, ivory, and ebony all have particular qualities that relate to wear, durability, smoothness of operation, and cosmetics, but shouldn't be chosen for tone enhancement (others may disagree).

A "zero" fret, or a fret positioned to replace the nut as a start to the scale length, is merely a taller fret than the rest of the frets. Zero frets are mostly found on inexpensive guitars as a cost-cutting move, but higher-end guitars are rediscovering its function. The fact that it is made from the same material as all the other frets leads to the logical conclusion that it is the most consistent tone between open and fretted strings. It has its drawbacks in that it is difficult to adjust for the best open string height above the first fret.

SADDLE

CASE 13:

"The action is too low, so I put a toothpick under the saddle to raise it and now the intonation is off and I see a crack forming along the saddle slot."

The saddle adjustment is the final piece to complete the action setup. If the frets are in alignment (see the fret section), the nut and truss rod are in adjustment, and the string height is high, then the saddle bottom or top is sanded or filed to achieve proper action. If the string height is too low, the saddle can be raised with a piece of flat wood or other well-fit hard shim material, or replaced if the shim is so tall that it causes the saddle to tip forward.

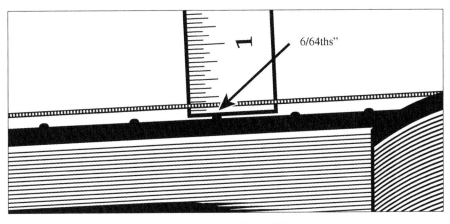

6/64ths"

Measuring string height at 12th fret

To gauge the height of the strings above the fretboard:

- measure the string height at the halfway, or 12th fret
- place a 6" ruler with 1/64" increments on end on top of the fret and observe where it meets the bottom of the string.

An ideal measurement is 6/64" at the low E and 4/64" at the high E.

Saddle slot depth is very important in determining the course of action as it relates to saddle height. Before any adjustments are made, the slot must be examined for any type of shim that may have been inserted under the saddle. A shallow slot will not support a saddle that is two or more thicknesses taller than the bridge height. A shallow slot and a high saddle—especially a loose-fitting one—will cause it to lean forward, creating a distorted slot and sharp intonation. Forward leverage exerted by a tall saddle can also result in a cracked bridge (see illustration).

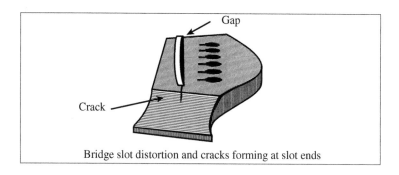

Bridge slot distortion and cracks forming at slot ends

CASE 14:

"How come the action feels high but there is string buzz, especially on the D and G strings?"

An often-overlooked setup detail is the saddle-to-fretboard radius relationship. It is typical to find a mismatched saddle radius causing setup problems from a larger radius of the saddle than the fretboard. In essence, the string height as measured at the 12th fret will be closer in the center of the fretboard than the outside strings. This is especially perplexing if you are measuring the string height of the outside strings only. This radius mismatch is usually because a repair person, or even the manufacturer of the guitars hadn't thought of the importance of this detail. Another reason is, if the saddle bottom is

30

cupped in a concave manner, when full string tension is applied, the saddle buckles and its radius flattens. Over-radiused saddles can have the opposite problem of outer strings being closer to the fingerboard than the inner strings (see illustration).

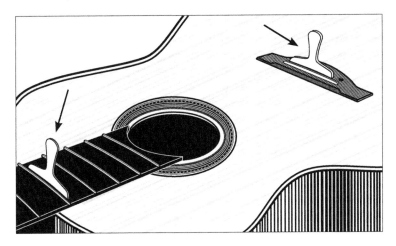

Saddle-to-fretboard radius matching using a radius gauge

A properly adjusted saddle top is always matched to the fretboard radius with a radius gauge.

CASE 15:

"I heard that changing the bridge saddle from Micarta
to bone will improve the tone of my guitar."

Much has been said about choosing saddle material as it relates to tone. Bone, graphite, Teflon, Micarta, and TUSQ saddles are all acceptable and all of the synthetic materials manufacturers insist that theirs improves tone or durability. The only exception is soft plastic found on some inexpensive guitars. Soft plastic doesn't stand up to forward string leverage and string wear. Most of the decision, by a large guitar manufacturer with respect to choosing a particular man-made material is based more on consistency, durability, and workability.

My experience has told me that proper fit of any hard material is more important to tone than the actual material. Too tight a fit and the projection and clarity may suffer slightly. Too loose a fit causes intonation problems or, in few cases, indistinct clarity. A cheap guitar has a lot of bad design elements. Replacing such a small part like a saddle by changing hard plastic to bone will have little discernable tonal effect. However, some people insist differing materials for the saddle and nut does change the guitar's overall tone. Conversely, an expensive, well-designed boutique guitar should sound good no matter what kind of saddle is in the bridge. This illuminates the fact that the choice of guitar woods, dimensioning, and finishing play more of a role than the saddle or nut materials. The bridge routinely contains hard organic materials like bone, fossilized bone, or ivory that wear well and are easily burnished to create a pleasing aesthetic. Subtle differences may be heard with different materials in under-saddle pickup response as it couples with a particular transducer or piezo element strip. As a side note, because I hear this query often, the addition of these types of under-saddle pickups, if properly installed, hardly affects acoustic tone.

To review, here is the order of adjustments: check neck relief, then the nut height, and finally the saddle height.

NTONATION

e mystery finally demystified

CASE 16:

"I can't keep my guitar in tune.
No matter what I do, I'm always tuning it.
Maybe I need new tuning machines."

Tuning machines are most often not the cause of tuning problems. If the saddle placement is wrong and/or the truss rod and string height are out of adjustment, no amount of tuning will correct faulty intonation. When determining what the problem is, be aware that two different elements are at work. The phrase "staying in tune" has one definition, although it is common to mix it up with "intonation":

- If the string is slipping or the string drifts after playing for a while, then it is not "staying in tune."

- If you are constantly tuning because chords or notes in the first position are different than the same notes in the second or third positions, then this is an intonation problem, not a tuning problem.

It is critical to be methodical in assessing the trio of adjustments before thinking there is something inherently wrong with your guitar as it relates to intonation or "staying in tune."

Replacing old strings is definitely the first place to start if you have tuning problems. Only worn and wiggling tuning gears or sealed machines with obvious glitches that are hard to adjust will cause difficulty in trying to fine tune and will ultimately need replacement.

Saddle placement is determined by scale length. The measurement is roughly twice the distance from the front edge of the nut to the center of the 12th fret. All steel-string guitars need compensation or intonation correction at the saddle. This is why you see a slant at the saddle slot. The thicker and higher-set low E string needs more compensation, or setback than the thinner and lower-set high E string. Higher action needs longer (or more) compensation, but a general rule that works well with all standard 25-1/2" scale-length guitars (a typical Martin dreadnought) is to add 1/16" to the treble side and 3/16" to the bass side. If this measurement doesn't prove to help a guitar with bad intonation, then most likely there are other setup adjustments to check concerning the nut, truss rod, and saddle as previously outlined. High action due to a high saddle or an excessively bowed neck always causes the string to play sharp (see illustration).

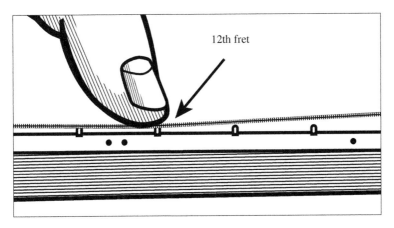

12th fret

Depressing a string stretches a string, ultimately sharping the note

CASE 17:

"I got a new compensated saddle installed in my guitar and I still have trouble with keeping it in tune up the neck."

It is customary to see guitars with compensated saddles as a hallmark of better intonation, but it isn't always the case. The slot location, if not ideally set, will influence the fixed compensated saddle. Factory-made, generic compensated saddles (saddle tops with different forward and back configurations, with the B string stepped back the furthest) might actually aggravate good intonation when compared to a standard non-compensated saddle. Every guitar has a general saddle-position setting, but determining factors like higher- or lower-than-standard truss rod and string-height adjustments, influence saddle location.

NECK ANGLE

Nothing to do with your head,
everything to do with playability

If the guitar action, or string height, is too high and the saddle is adjusted down to the minimum 1/16" above the top of the bridge (there must be string-break angle over the top of the saddle or tone and volume will suffer) then a decision must be made by a luthier with respect to either reducing the bridge and saddle height or changing the neck angle to regain lower action and proper saddle-height-to-bridge ratio. The ideal height of the saddle above the bridge is 1/8" to 3/16" above the full-height 3/8" bridge.

To estimate whether your guitar has an acceptable neck angle, lay a 24" straightedge accross the fretboard, near the front edge of the nut, and note where it comes to rest at the bridge. If the bridge is higher than 3/8" then shaving the bridge down might be an acceptable alternative. Ideally, the ruler should come to rest on top of the original bridge while touching the entire fretboard (make sure the bridge has not already been shaved down below the minimum 5/16"). The only caveat is that the neck must be straight, especially where the upper end of the fretboard is in relation to the lower end. If the high end of the fretboard (14th fret and higher) kicks up at the fingerboard extension, it will give a false reading by making the straightedge rest higher on the bridge than it really is. This is why a sighting of the neck in combination with the ruler test is a good idea (see illustration).

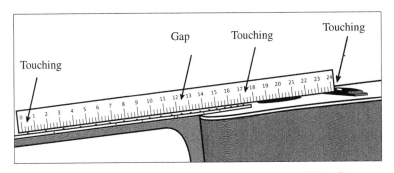

End of fretboard tipping the ruler up giving a false neck angle reading

Conversely, too steep an angle causes the high saddle or the tall bridge height to put undo forward and upward leverage on the top. This causes bridges and braces to detach, the bridge to crack along the pin holes, or the top to warp, leading to intonation problems.

CASE 18:

"I don't understand why my guitar needs a neck reset. It always had good action and I haven't played it in 20 years. It just sat in my closet strung up like the day I put it away."

Neck-angle change via neck removal and reset is common on older instruments or instruments originally made with shallow neck angles (low bridges under 5/16" with minimal saddle protruding) or guitars left in cases with full string tension left on, especially in inhospitable conditions. The constant string pressure left on a guitar for years eventually pulls and stretches the wood fiber, which leads to neck-angle shift as it pivots at the neck heel.

Neck removal procedures vary greatly, depending on who made the guitar. Some guitars, like Martins, produce guitars with dovetail joins that are easily removed. With proper technique, a qualified luthier can remove, shim, recut, reset and install a neck in a day's time.

Taylor guitars (except for earlier models) are even easier to remove because they are secured with three bolts and incorporate a shim system that enables a luthier to drop in different size shims instead of gluing and cutting the neck heel to affect a change. Earlier models with two bolts and a glued-on fretboard extension are demarcated by the Taylor label, with the serial number affixed to the neck block. Later, three-bolt models have paper labels affixed to the back with the serial number, with another label at the neck block with only "Taylor" printed on it.

Gibson and Guild guitars are more difficult to reset. Unlike Martin, or other guitars with the body and neck finished separately, their necks and bodies are finished together causing more work in retouching the broken finish line.

Private makers, as well as some imports, have different methods of attachment.

- Gurian guitars made in the '60s and '70s employ ebony pegs that wedge-fit to hold the neck to the neck block, making a glueless and boltless join.
- David Russell Young, a very popular maker in the '70s, epoxied many of his necks on.
- Guitars like Hofner and Framus employ a very shallow violin-type, non-dovetailed mortise and tenon.

Less expensive Ovation guitars epoxy their necks on.

Each type of joinery and choice of glue presents differing methods of removal—and some are made not to be reset. Traditional classical guitars employ a "Spanish Foot," which is an extension of the neck, meaning there is no separate neck block. Removal of a portion of the back to "slip" the back over the foot and reattaching with binding and back trimming is one method employed to change the neck angle. Another, more typical method is to replace the fingerboard with a wedge-shaped one or inserting a wedge under the existing fingerboard. Bear this in mind before assuming all guitars are built to have reversible neck joinery.

MORE FACTS

TUNING MACHINES

Machines, tuning heads, tuning pegs, machine heads, tuners…they're all the same.

CASE 19:

"Every time I tune a string, I hear a pinging noise and it skips past where the string needs to be in order to be in tune. I think I need new tuners."

Sealed-gear tuning machines like Grover, Gotoh, and Schaller are seldom the cause of tuning problems. Soft plastic nuts are the most prone to this annoyance, but any type of nut will create this problem if the string grooves aren't properly filed. Tuning glitches like this sometimes are equated to a faulty tuning machine, though it is not the case.

Opened-gear tuners are of varying quality, from old three-on-a-side Grover Sta-Tite to the newly improved Grover Vintage and Waverly. Three-on-a-plate-type open-gear tuners are usually not of the highest quality, although there are reproductions that are much improved from the originals. The cheaper versions are prone to excessive "backlash," which affects the feel of the tuner. The looseness makes it difficult to zero in on the right pitch. Older, worn gears will definitely make the guitar more difficult to tune because the tolerances are so large between the cog and worm gear that it is only possible to tune as you turn up, not down, to the desired note. Backlash can be tested on any type of machine-open or sealed tuner by first removing the string, gripping the tuning post with thumb and forefinger, and turning the string post clockwise and then quickly counterclockwise in a jiggling, back and forth motion. A worn machine has an obvious amount of play between turns. Another test for looseness is to pull the post up and down on an unstrung machine and feel for excessive movement (see illustration on next page).

Stiff open-geared tuners are greatly improved with a light application of machine oil at all friction points (see illustration).

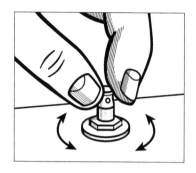

Testing for backlash

Oil Here

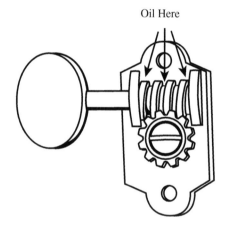

STRINGS AND STRING CHANGING

**Most guitarists were never really taught
how to restring a guitar…**

CASE 20:

*"I'm having trouble staying in tune.
I haven't changed all the strings in a couple
of months, just the ones I've broken."*

Change strings when either intonation falters, strings don't seem to stay in tune, or their tone is dull and lifeless. The amount of time between string changes is anywhere from one week to many months. Factors that shorten or extend these times are:

- Certain hand acids that kill string resonance

- Steel-string rusting

- The frequency of playing

- How often you play after eating greasy food with your hands!

Many string makers now offer coated strings that prolong string life. Trying different brands is a good idea in order to find which set sounds best on any particular guitar. I always recommend light-gauge strings (.012"-.053") because they exert a moderate amount of tension, which is best for the life of a lightly built resonant guitar. Medium-gauge strings (013."-.056") are also acceptable, but some guitars are not capable of holding up to the extra tension. The end results are bridge detachment and top warping. Heavily braced and thickly topped instruments can react favorably to medium-gauge. Always check with a luthier before deciding to step up to medium gauge.

I've seen many older guitars that, because they were always strung with medium-gauge strings, needed neck resets prematurely and suffered top distortions with accompanying separated braces. Always use light-gauge strings first before settling on the extra tension supplied by the heavier medium strings. Some lightly built guitars can't take the extra 15 pounds of tension from medium strings. Some guitars built earlier than the 1920s were never meant to have strings heavier then gut (nylon.) If you're uncertain about which string to use, consult a knowledgeable luthier or vintage instrument dealer. Using too heavy a string can not only rip the bridge off, but can splinter the top and cause brace and top distortion.

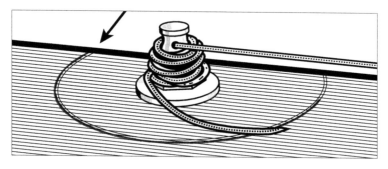

Loose ends and too many string windings can mar a head stock

I'm continually surprised by how many accomplished guitarists string their guitars poorly. I see knots tied and way too many windings on the tuning posts. Besides being very difficult to restring quickly, like when a string breaks at a gig, the multiple windings put strain on the tuners and alter string-break angle off of the nut. Strings cut with too much hanging off the end can put deep scratches in the headstock veneer, leaving circular gouges around string posts (see above illustration). Depending on how high the string post and string hole are above the peghead, there should be no more than three or four windings and they should be evenly coiled from the top to the bottom of the shaft, with the strings cut closely to the machine post. The reverse lock is the most secure and easiest method to unstring (see illustration).

Direction of post to tighten string

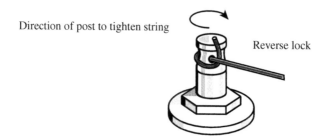

Reverse lock

Example of treble-side tuner string lock

On steel-string acoustic guitars, make sure the ball end of the string is firmly seated under the bridge by pushing down on the bridge pin while pulling up on the string (see illustration).

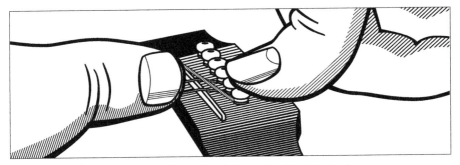

Pull up with left hand, push down pin with right thumb

CASE 21:

"When I changed my strings, I increased the string gauge from light to medium so I could get more volume from my guitar. It didn't do much, so I wondered whether going to an even heavier gauge would give me more volume?"

What you will get if you go to a heavier gauge is a higher, stiffer action, possibly an unglued bridge, and wrist and finger pain!

Going to a medium string gauge will sometimes diminish volume as the top struggles to respond to the extra tension, causing a bit of an overdriven "pinched" tone. This is especially apt to occur on a guitar with a thinly dimensioned top and light bracing.

It is worth trying a medium gauge on a heavily and thickly braced top, but don't expect miracles.

One way I test to see whether a top, is thin or thick is to press firmly on the top in various places behind the bridge where most vibration occurs. If it yields easily to downward thumb pressure, I would caution against increasing string gauge.

Increasing string gauge may help to alleviate fret buzz if the picking attack is strong.

CASE 22:

"I never change strings by taking them all off at the same time because I heard it can harm the guitar."

That is a myth that I hear continually repeated. No string damage will occur by realeasing all string tension before resuming restringing.

Here are a few pointers as you begin restringing:

- I wouldn't cut all of the strings off at once with full string tension on. This could shock the guitar, pluck out an eye, or inflict damage to the top via string whip.

- Replacing one string at a time with the rest at full tension helps stabilize tuning.

- Removing all the strings makes it easy to clean and oil the fretboard and buff the frets with steel wool.

STRAP BUTTONS
Where to screw them without screwing up the neck.

Most new guitars don't have a strap button at the neck heel. Strap buttons can be seen as being in the way, especially if attached too close to the fretboard. Have a qualified luthier install one as needed. Problems arise when a do-it-yourselfer installs one without knowing where to place it or what size drill bit to use and how deep to drill. Location is vital for balance and how it affects the frethand placement. Drilling into guitars with a one- or two-bolt neck attachment requires careful measuring so as not to drill into the bolts. This can cause premature failure of the bolt's metal-threaded insert or cracking of the neck itself.

The alternative is tying the strap behind the nut. Most people find this way of attachment hinders hand movement, however.

END PINS

**One little piece of plastic—and one disaster
in the making if it fits too loosely.**

CASE 23:

*"My end pin came out. I wrapped some masking
tape around to hold it. It's still holding!"*

Most guitars come with a tapered end pin or a screwed-in metal strap button.

Wrapping tape around the pin to help hold in a loose end pin is fine as a temporary measure, but dried-out tape can let go suddenly, causing the guitar to come crashing to the floor. Finding an oversized end pin is a possibility, but most are standard size. I have replaced plastic end pins with ebony or rosewood viola end pins, as they are larger than standard pins. The hole must first be enlarged to accept the larger pin and might not cosmetically match the existing bridge pins.

Even common end-pin jacks are notorious for dropping guitars (when the guitar is not plugged in) because their size is too large and not compatible with most strap holes. Thick, soft leather straps are particularly vulnerable to coming off. Enlarging the hole to match the end-pin diameter helps it to stay on.

BUYING A USED GUITAR
Too many guitars, too many bad deals.

CASE 24:

"I found a guitar on eBay that looked good in the picture. It's a Gibson, so I know it had to be worth more than the $400 I paid for it. It seems that it needs some minor adjustments because the action is really high and it's buzzing a lot."

Unless you plan on a home repair or spending more money for a qualified repair person, stay away from internet finds that appear too good to be true. Damaged instruments that are in need of repair are one thing; a bad repair is almost always harder to repair than if it was left in its original state. I don't care what the bluebook price says a guitar is worth. After bad and nonreversible repairs are done, the guitar has lost most of its value.

Besides the obvious cosmetic considerations (i.e., visible wear and overall tone), the most important aspect of deciding whether to buy a used guitar is its ability to be adjusted for playable action. This is directly related to the neck's relationship to the body, or neck angle. Sight-unseen purchases on websites of used guitars from private sellers are problematic because you can't see and feel the playability as it relates to neck angle. The problem is compounded if the seller has no clue as to what constitutes good action. I would avoid any purchase unless you have worked out a deal between you and the seller that enables you to take it to a trusted luthier and have it thoroughly checked out before final purchase. It is customary to have at least a 48-hour grace period for such a reason. Before purchasing, consider the following:

If the action is good but the bridge is hardly higher than 1/4" with the saddle just barely standing off the bridge top, then future adjustments to lower the action can't be made. If this scenario also includes high action, then the guitar will need a neck reset.

Neck resetting is the single most expensive maintenance repair on guitars with glued dovetail joins. If the bridge has already been cut down, the bridge will have to be replaced to achive its original height in order to regain future saddle adjustments. Refretting is a consideration because the upper fretboard is now newly aligned to the body, causing a shift at the neck/body join. Costs vary on a traditional dovetail-neck-joined guitar, ranging anywhere from $275 to $500. Bolt-on necks are much easier to reset, so costs are lower (see the Neck Angle section).

Assess the structure by raking light across the entire instrument—most importantly, the top. By this I mean holding the instrument in strong light, especially sunlight that reflects light in a way that its angle better reveals the surface structure. This will expose any dips, creases, and bulges. Creases signify cracks that are forming or old crack repairs. Dips signify loose braces or poorly reglued braces (see the Humidity section). The only way to really tell internal problems is to use an inspection mirror and internal light source.

For frets that are deeply notched from string wear and are loose or have uneven frets that have to be leveled or replaced, figure another $100-$300 for repair.

Check that the bridge is securely glued to the top. Make sure that full string tension is on during the inspection. See if the bridge has been reglued. If you see a ghost line of the original bridge placement, the intonation will most likely be off.

Check for any headstock cracks or old glued cracks. The common area to inspect is just under the truss-rod channel on the back of the neck, if indeed the adjustment nut is at the headstock. This is a place that commonly breaks because truss-rod channels remove a good amount of wood, which decreases wood strength in this critical, high-stress area.

Small side or back cracks are inconsequential as it relates to structural integrity. It is only a concern if they are long or wide enough to see daylight through them, in which case the string tension will eventually cause them to pull the top and back apart.

Note any loose binding. Old guitars with brittle and crumbling binding that need to be replaced is a costly job, as it requires finish touch-up.

CLEANING AND POLISHING
It's the least you can do.

CASE 25:

"I can't seem to clean the top of my guitar where my arm rests. My guitar polish doesn't do anything but make it worse."

Before using any kind of spray polish, the surface must be free of grime or greasy residue. Spraying polish over a sweat-smeared, grimy surface will only make it more unmanageable. Cigarette smoke residue covering grime is particularly tenacious and hard to remove. A more aggressive cleaner must be used before any final polish. Meguiar's #2 Fine-Cut Cleaner, available from car parts stores and auto-finishing websites, does a good job of removing dirt without abrading the finish like a car compound will. Over-zealous rubbing may still rub through a fragile older finish. Restore cleaner from Planet Waves is similar, although it is less aggressive.

Using a car-finish compound is not recommended unless the finish is urethane, catalyzed, or polyester. Gibson, Martin, and U.S.A. made Guild, for example, use a softer nitrocellulose lacquer. Expensive boutique guitars are usually finished in either nitrocellulose or shellac. This type of finish and older shellac-based or spirit-varnished instruments require a studied hand if you want to remove just dirt, not finish.

Only after all grime and dirt are removed can a guitar polish be used. Remember: you are polishing lacquer, not wood, so don't use any oil-based products on the finish. Besides the fact that oil doesn't shine lacquer, it can seep into minute cracks in the finish, staining the wood. Oil like lemon oil should only be used on unfinished fretboards and bridges. I use a lemon oil/beeswax compound so it is thicker than mere lemon oil, thereby filling the wood pores and leaving a waxy, protective coating.

Guitars with matte finishes can't be cleaned with anything more than a damp cloth. Using any type of polish may result in splotchy shiny spots.

THE 12-STRING GUITAR

CASE 26:

*"I bought a new 12-string guitar and within a
year the action got so high I couldn't play it"*

Twelve-string guitars are under a tremendous amount of string tension. A light-gauge set exerts about 252 pounds of pull, and extra lights about 218 pounds (a six-string set of light-gauge strings exerts 155 pounds of tension).

In its first year, any new guitar can go through an action change requiring truss rod or saddle adjustments. Given the increased string tension, 12-string guitar action can be even more extreme. I always recommend using extra-light-gauge strings to reduce tension unless the guitar top is sufficiently braced and its truss rod is capable of withstanding the force of light or medium gauge.

CASE 27:

*"I have a 12-string that I use only
occasionally, but every time I pull it out of its
case it seems the action has to be adjusted lower."*

Unless you are an avid 12-string player, you have to pay close attention to its care. Storing a 12-string guitar for more than a few months without releasing a bit of string tension by detuning a whole step can result in neck-angle change, as well as neck-bow, bridge-lift, and top distortion. Don't store the guitar in an unheated attic or moist basement. Check on the action occasionally if you really aren't going to play it for the better part of a year.

Don't release full string tension without first loosening the truss rod approximately a full turn, or else you could end up with a back-bowed neck. Remember: the truss rod is counteracting the tension that a full set of 12 strings is exerting.

Twelve-string guitar action is generally set lower at the saddle with a slightly straighter neck relief than a six-string. This helps facilitate barre chording. I measure 5/64" on bass side and 3/64" on treble side at the 12th fret.

UKULELES

The best thing about ukuleles from a player standpoint is that the short scale length combined with four low-tensioned nylon strings makes for the easiest playing of all fretted string instruments. Even ukes with poor neck angle are playable at the first position.

CASE 28:

"I want to play the ukulele but don't know what size to buy. And how do you tune it?"

Here are the sizes (based on Martin ukuleles) as measured across the widest point across the top at the lower bout:

- Soprano: 6-3/8"
- Concert: 7-5/8"
- Tenor: 8-5/16"
- Baritone: 10"

As one would guess, the smaller the uke, the less sound projection, although higher-quality soprano ukes can be surprisingly robust. Tunings, from bass to treble, on the soprano, concert, and tenor sizes are most commonly G–C–E–A. The baritone is tuned like the top four strings of a guitar: D–G–B–E

ARCHTOP GUITARS

By way of design, archtop, cello, or carved-top guitars produce sound differently than flat-top instruments. As the name implies, the tops and usually the backs of these guitars have arches carved into them from thick pieces of wood (less expensive archtops may have their arches steam pressed rather than carved). The arching resists the downward force of the strings, as they are secured from a tailpiece rather than from the upward force of a pin bridge.

CASE 29:

"Why is the intonation on my archtop guitar good sometimes and bad other times? I positioned my bridge where the wear marks from the bridge are on the guitar top."

Poorly coupled bridge-top-to-base configuration makes for an unstable bridge. Other factors that affect intonation are undersized, wobbly bridge tops perched on string adjuster posts that are too short, causing forward tilt from string pressure.

Archtop bridges have a tendency to move because they are not glued to the top. **Important note:** Don't rely on positioning of the bridge based on marks on the top from where the bridge had been. Always check with a tuner for exact intonation placement.

This brings up the concept of good bridge design. Like all guitars, neck angle has an important role to play in bridge height. With good neck angle, a tall bridge 1" to 1-1/4" will produce better tone and stability than a short bridge. The tailpiece holds the strings and also keeps string tension on the bridge. The bridge can stay in place only if the neck angle is steep enough to secure it. With good neck angle, a firmly coupled dense wood bridge like ebony helps with tone and stability. Bridge bases need to be sanded to match the archtop curvature.

If the neck angle is steep, the bridge should accommodate the increased height by beefing up both the top and bridge base. Assuming the bridge is a two-piece and adjustable with thumbwheels, the best bridge design is one that couples the top and base so there is little-to-no space between them. A tall and thinly dimensioned bridge top jacked up high on string adjusting posts creates three problems:

- Tone suffers as string energy is dissipated, as it is directed mostly through the adjusting posts
- Instability is the result of forward push from string tension
- Warping and possible cracking of the bridge top

(See illustrations on following page.)

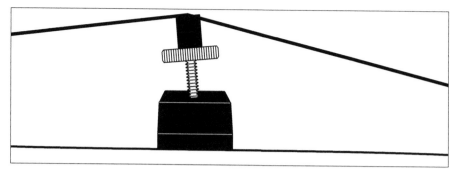

Keep an eye on forward tilt due to tuning up,
which pushes the bridge top forward

Bridge bottom conforming to guitar top, with little or
no space between bridge top and base

THE CLASSICAL GUITAR

Before identifying different aspects of classical guitar construction as it relates to steel-string construction, please make sure to read the book's first two topics, Humidity and Cracks. The choices of woods used in both styles of guitar are similar, therefore they will react similarly when exposed to the environment. Rosewood or mahogany back and side wood and cedar, spruce, or even redwood for top wood are interchangeable between guitar types. The dissimilarity in fretboard thicknesses between the two types of guitars accounts for the tendency of the thicker classical fretboard to pull cracks into the top alongside the fretboard extension. This is a fault of the unstable ebony fretboard shrinking from dryness and taking the softer top wood with it as it loses dimension.

The classical guitar, or generically known as the "nylon-string guitar," is different than the steel-string guitar in some major ways:

- The neck width at the nut is wide, measuring up to 2-1/8" as opposed to the narrower steel-string neck which is typically 1-5/8". This facilitates complicated finger movements on both the fretting hand and the plucking hand. The majority of classical guitars have flat fretboards as opposed to the radiused steel-string fretboard.

- The top-bracing array is also much different due to the fact that a standard set of nylon strings has about 85 pounds of tension at standard pitch as opposed to the 165 pounds for steel strings. For this reason, the construction is both lighter in weight and bracing is thinner and typically arranged in a fan pattern, or Torres style, under the bridge area, unlike the heavier X-brace of the steel string (see illustrations on next page).

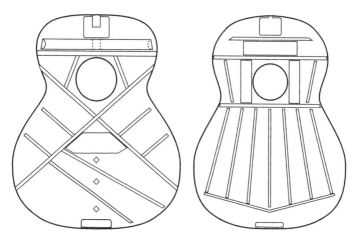

Although there are many bracing designs, these are the most common

- More guitar makers are employing a lattice brace system both for tone and for symmetrical strength. This system avoids the common distorted-top pitfalls from the rotating action at the bridge due to string tension of the Torres fan system.

- Because of the lighter string tension and more supple strings, the string height on a classical is set higher above the fretboard. Concert performers who don't use amplification have their action set very high to help with volume and projection. I have set string heights as high as 12/64" at the 12th fret. Less demanding players usually have a lower height set, maybe 7/64" to 8/64" at the 12th fret.

- Stringing the classical is different at both the bridge and the tuning gears (see illustration).

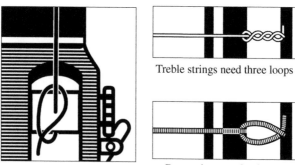

Treble strings need three loops

Bass strings need only one

THE HYBRID NYLON-STRING GUITAR

The hybrid nylon string is basically a classical-sized body coupled with a thinner steel-string neck usually includes a radiused fretboard. Some versions have a neck width somewhere between the two extremes, yet maintaining the flat fretboard. Other additions are a cutaway at the treble side upper bout and internal electronics. Jazz players, or others who like the classical sound and lighter string tension yet can't deal with the extra wide and flat fretboard, are ideally suited to this style.

THE FLAMENCO GUITAR

The flamenco guitar is a much lighter-built classical-size, guitar that usually uses less dense woods. Spanish cedar neck wood, Spanish cypress (a kind of evergreen tree with fine grain and light weight), and most typically spruce or Spanish pine soundboard are the first choices. The reasons for these woods reflect, first, what was native wood at the time of the original construction of the flamenco guitar in Spain in the late 19th century and, presently, what has become the "flamenco sound." Unlike classical guitar, with its richer tone and more sustain, the flamenco is known for its short sustain and percussive attack described as a "dry" sound. Originally, the flamenco guitar was used as an accompanist's instrument for vocal and dance. Now it is also known as a solo instrument. The late Paco de Lucia was one of the first and most well-known flamenco guitarist to elevate the instrument to the concert halls of Spain and, later, worldwide. Because of his quest for more tonal variations, he popularized the rosewood side and back variant called the "flamenco negra."

THE CASE FOR CASES

If you want to preserve your guitar, protect it during travel and keep a buffer between it and the environment, get a good hard shell case. I can't stress this enough.

During harsh drying winters, a well-humidified case is a micro climate for your guitar. Keep it closed even when you are using the guitar so it preserves the moister environment you hopefully have created. Using a case hygrometer is a must as it is the only sure way to monitor humidity levels (see Humidity section).

If you use a soft bag instead of a hard-shell case, it is harder to retain consistent humidity. It is also less likely that you will return the guitar to the case after use because it is more of a hassle to deal with than a latching case. This sets you up to leave the guitar leaning against a wall or on a bed or guitar stand where not only are you exposing it to dry air, but you are making it easier to knock over and create broken headstock, scrapes, dents, and cracks.

A flimsy chipboard case is also less desirable than a hard-shell case for obvious reasons. The worst part of these cases are when the internally glued-flocked material coverings that are over the metal hinges, clasps and handles eventually dry up and fall off, exposing sharp metal rivets. These scrape off the guitar finish, especially on older, thinner finishes.

All hardshell cases are not always a good fit, so you must make sure the case isn't so tight as to cause side pressure cracks or so loose that the guitar is bouncing around.

- One dangerous condition is if the neck brace is too tall, causing the headstock to come in contact with the case top. This is especially bad if the neck brace is also too close to the guitar body, causing excess pressure on the neck heel and fretboard-to-neck joinery at the first fret area.

- Old and worn cases with short neck braces are equally bad because the headstock is in a position to take all of the pressure at the weakest point at the back of the neck just behind the nut. Guitars that have truss-rod channels at the headstock are especially vulnerable to the short neck-brace problem.

On an older case it is easy to tell either of these conditions by examining the inner case fabric for tuning post dents on the top or tuning machine or headstock wear on the case bottom.

A well-designed case will be snug around the body, with a neck support keeping the neck at an angle where the back is lying on the case bottom and the neck is gently cradled. You should see a slight depression by the bridge pins and strings on the case top. If the case is new and you aren't sure if it is too big for the guitar, open the guitar case and strum across all the strings. When you close the case, you should hear the vibrating-strings-sound stop.

PICKUPS
The Big Decision:
Should I put a pickup in my acoustic guitar?

I would think twice before electrifying a vintage guitar, especially if it is a high-end guitar like a pre-war Martin in relatively good condition. The problem is mostly the drilling out of the end-pin hole to accept the end-pin jack. The size of a standard end-pin jack requires a 15/32" hole to be drilled through the existing end-pin hole. There are smaller standard end-pin-like jacks that take a smaller 1/8" inch cable connection, but these jacks are not the best with respect to strength and conductivity.

If a client asks me about pickups before he or she buys a guitar, I first suggest buying a guitar with a factory-installed pickup system. This way, there is no guesswork when determining what kind of electrical quality it will lend to your instrument.

I am continually asked whether a pickup will affect the acoustic tone of a guitar. I say it is not true, but a botched installation of an under-saddle pickup or if not enough saddle is left after accounting for the pickup sensor's thickness or a saddle-slot problem or a string-to-saddle mismatch may affect, very minimally, the tonal projection.

My quibble with some aftermarket installations are that there are too many wires, a battery holder, a preamp, and volume controls, making it a bit of an internal mess. Guitars like Martin and Taylor, and many import guitars, have well-thought-out pickup systems that are integral to the guitar. The only downside might be a change in attitude towards the factory electric sound, and therefore you want to change to an aftermarket pickup that can't be adapted to the existing holes in the guitar.

If you do decide to add a pickup to an all-acoustic guitar, I suggest one of these three types of pickups:

- If you are a coffee-house-type solo player favoring fingerstyle technique, an unpowered transducer like the K+K Pure Western Mini is a fine choice. It reproduces the guitar's inherent acoustic qualities more than some others. I've installed more than 150 of them in the eight years I have been using them. They sense sound in a way that is more like a microphone. Herein lies its only problem, unless preamped: If they reach a certain high volume, they tend to sound boomy. If you add an external preamp, you can control the unwanted "boxy" sound.

- The Amulet System is similar in its pickup placement to the unpowered transducer but it has an internal preamp end pin. It is clear and strong sounding. It is pricier than the K&K and requires a more involved installation procedure.

- If you are more of a strumming guitarist in an electrified band with drums, you will find that a powered under-saddle pickup has more volume headroom and cutting power. Its drawback is that it makes the guitar sound more electric. The under-saddle piezo element senses sound by contact pressure between saddle and sensor. For this reason, the mating of the two must be near perfect. The saddle slot must also be trued so that there are no high or low spots. Uneven response between strings is not uncommon, especially if not installed by someone with experience.

- Soundhole pickups are another option. They can be installed semi-permanently with an end-pin jack or temporarily without an end pin jack if you don't mind the cable hanging off the pickup. Fishman and L.R. Baggs are good choices.

I find that, if a combo system (mic with under-saddle) is installed, the amount of mic used ends up being minimal, favoring about 85% piezo, or feedback will occur.

Unfortunately, with all the choices available, trying to find, by trial and error, the best-sounding pickup for your guitar can be an expensive hobby.

You must never underestimate the inherent acoustic qualities as it relates to electric transmission. Some big bass-dominant dreadnoughts may be more limited as to which type of pickup to use, whereas smaller-bodied instruments with less bottom end may act more favorably to a greater variety of pickups.

You must also never underestimate what your guitar is plugged into. Amplifiers and P.A. sound systems add their own unique tonal characteristics. Trying a guitar at a music store through an expensive acoustic guitar amp will sound different than an electric guitar amp. Impedence matching pickup to amp is important. Electromagnetic pickups have different impedence than piezo or transducer types.

Playing at home is different than playing in a large room for many people. Once volume levels increase, air volume of your guitar starts to come into play, more adding another level of tone change. A graphic equalizer and preamp always help to control unwanted bass, midrange, and treble peaks.

ODDS AND ENDS
Tuner Buttons

When tuner buttons on sealed gear machines are loose, check to see if a nylon washer on the button shaft is split or missing. A wavy metal washer could also be missing. Compounding this problem is if either washer is missing or broken, the tuner-button adjusting screw will, in some cases, be too long. Shortening the screw will make it tighten fully, but replacing the washers must be done first.

Strings Hanging Up in the Nut

Assess a binding nut by pushing down on the string between tuner post and nut. A non-binding nut will stay in tune after depressing and relaxing. If the string detunes, it is binding.

Stuck Bridge Pin

To release a stuck bridge pin, cut the string within 3" of the bridge with a wire cutter. Gripping the string with the cutters an inch from the bridge pin hole, push the string down into the hole, releasing the string from the pin.

Changing Strings

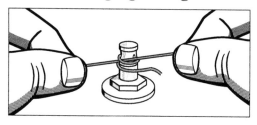

If a broken string fragment is caught in the string post, use the new string end to thread through the broken string, popping it out of the post hole (see illustration).

The best reason to change strings is if:

- there is visible string wear
- they sound dead
- there is a dissonant or indistinct buzz
- intonation is faulty.

Guitar Straps

Always check the guitar-strap fit on end-pin jacks. The jack ends are wider than most precut strap holes. Widening the strap hole to fit over the strap jack is a remedy.

Don't tighten loose strap-jack end caps without first removing the cap and inserting an awl or nail into the barrel hole to keep the entire jack from spinning. Failure to keep the jack from spinning could lead to wires crossing, shorting the pickup or breaking the ground or lead wires (see illustration).

nail or awl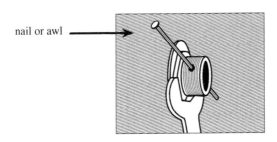

Broken String

Did you break a string near the tuner and you don't have the right replacement string? Use a Becket's sheet-bend knot to splice a string to the tuning post (see illustration)

Tape on a Guitar

Don't leave any masking or Scotch tape on guitars with nitrocellulose finishes for more than a week or two as it will react to the finish and become more difficult to remove the adhesive residue. Nitrocellulose lacquer finish is found on Martin and Gibson instruments.

TEST REVIEW

1. When restringing, you should never remove all strings at once.

2. Shimming a nut is a good way of adjust action when the action is low at the 12th fret.

3. A pre-compensated saddle will always correct intonation problems.

4. A pinging sound when tuning up strings is caused by a faulty tuning machine.

5. You should humidify your guitar all year long, no matter what the relative humidity is.

6. Adjusting the truss rod is the best way to lower or raise action.

7. To prevent string slippage, the more string windings on the tuning gear post the better.

8. A bridge that is separated from the top at the back edge by under an 1/8" should always be immediately reglued.

9. A loose top brace, not a loose back brace, is usually the cause of non-fret buzz.

ANSWERS

1. Removing all the strings will not harm the guitar, assuming you will be restringing it within a week or so. Leaving it unstrung without loosening the truss rod for extended periods could cause neck back-bow..

2. Nut height is determined after the truss rod is set. The final action is adjusted at the saddle.

3. Proper saddle location is easily determined, usually without the need for generic compensation.

4. Pinging noises emanating from the nut are either caused by soft plastic material or by the nut slots being too tight, not angled, or not cut well.

5. Once your house or apartment heating system shuts off for the year, remove the humidifier. Over-humidifying is bad for the guitar, as it raises action as it swells the top, pushing the fretboard extension up.

6. The truss rod affects the action but it should not be used as the only way to adjust action. Nut and saddle adjustments must be part of the overall action equation.

7. Too many windings add horizontal strain to the gears via the post and can cause the string's trajectory from the post to be too high, leading to bad down-pressure on the nut.

8. Remember that a bridge should only be reglued when absolutely necessary because some wood fiber is always lost during the regluing process.

9. Loose back braces are more likely to cause a weak resonance or indistinct tone as it relates to its reflective nature against the top's sound production.

TROUBLESHOOTING

I'm sure I missed a few

Condition	What is Happening	What to Do
1) High action	One or more of these conditions exist: • Saddle high • Top swollen (in humid months) • Neck bowed • Nut high • Neck loose at heel • Bridge pulling off	• Lower saddle • Blow dry case/store guitar in case • Tighten truss rod • File nut slots lower • Remove and reset neck/tighten bolts on bolt-on necks • Reglue bridge
2) String height high and saddle is at minimum height and truss rod is adjusted straight	• Neck angle is shifting due to poor original neck angle or neck wood stretch on older guitars or weak wood on newer guitars • Neck heel is coming loose from body	• Have neck angle reset to full-height bridge and saddle • Tighten bolts on bolt-on necks
3) Truss rod is tight and doesn't want to tighten further	• Either truss rod is at the end of its threads, the truss rod nut needs lubrication or it is truly as tight as it can go without breaking	• Take off truss-rod nut and lubricate with 3-in-1 oil and try again. Stop if the nut stops at the same point. May need backup washers to increase adjustability. May need neck heat warping

4) Intonation not true/Can't seem to stay in tune or tune guitar easily	One, some, or all of these conditions exist:	
	• String height too high	• Adjust saddle
	• Neck bowed	• Adjust truss rod
	• Bridge-saddle leaning	• Make new, tighter-fitting saddle
	• Saddle-slot distorted	• Fill slot with matching wood/Recut slot
	• Bridge in the wrong place	• Reglue oversized bridge in proper place or recut bridge slot
	• String not secure at tuning machine or bridge	• Review restringing technique
	• Loose tuning machine is holding down bushings	• Tighten bushings
	• Fret hand is pulling string down	• Correct playing technique
	• Neck loose or cracked	• Check carefully for any hairline cracks under nut
	• Old strings or defective new strings	• Change string(s)

Symptom	Cause	Solution
5) Strings won't stay in tune	• Strings not secure at string post or at bridge pins • Frets are dented from string wear	• Review restringing technique • Review #4
6) Fret buzz on open string only	• Nut slot cut too deeply, causing string to buzz off of the first fret	• Have nut replaced or shimmed
	• Fretboard unglued from neck at first fret area	• Re-glue fretboard
7) Fret buzz when note is fretted but buzz stops when string is damped behind fretted note	• Nut slot(s) cut too deeply causing string to buzz off of any fret between nut and fretted note	• Have nut replaced or shimmed • Truss rod too tight
	• Deeper fret wear on upper fretboard than lower	• Level frets
8) Fret buzz on chords between first and fifth frets	• Neck backbowed or frets ahead of buzz are higher than or out of alignment with lower frets. • Fret wear	• Adjust truss rod • Have fret-alignment checked • Level or replace frets
9) Fret buzz on upper fretboard only	• Neck-angle shift causing fretboard extension to be out of alignment with the rest of the fretboard	• Neck angle may need to change, or refret upper fretboard after it is first planed down to align with lower fretboard. • Check if board is unglued from top
	• Frets dented with string wear	• Level frets

Problem	Possible Cause	Solution
10) Fret buzz on random frets on the fretboard	• Saddle too low • Frets out of alignment • Loose frets • Dented or worn frets	• Shim or replace saddle • Have all frets secured and leveled
11) Fret buzz and/or dead, or poorly sustaining, notes	• Loose and/or dented and worn frets	• Have frets glued and leveled or replaced
12) Fret buzz on entire length of fretboard and on all strings (string height too low)	• Top collapsing from low humidity • Neck severely back-bowed • Saddle too low • Loose top bracing	• Rehydrate guitar • Loosen truss rod • Shim or replace with higher saddle • Reglue loose braces
13) Fret buzz along entire fretboard on one string yet adjacent strings don't buzz	• Old or even new string is faulty and not vibrating evenly	• Change string(s)
14) Non-fret buzz rattle or indistinct tonal clarity	• Loose back or top brace	• Have loose braces reglued
15) Metallic-sounding non-fret buzz	• Loose tuning machine bushing or gear mesh/loose tuner button/truss-rod cover loose/truss-rod nut loose/truss-rod shaft loose in truss-rod neck channel	• Tighten all loose parts • Glue may need to be injected into truss-rod channel

Problem	Cause	Solution
16) Can only tune up to pitch. If tuning down, string goes out of tune	• String is binding or not sized properly in nut slot	• Have nut slot(s) recut
	• Tuning machine is worn out	• Check tuner backlash (see illustration in Tuning Machines section)
17) Breaking same string repeatedly	• If string is breaking at the saddle, it may be too sharply beveled.	• Examine saddle top and sand smooth
	• String is at too steep a break angle from pin hole	• Make sure string height is not too high or bridge is too steep
	• Picking attack is too aggressive for chosen string gauge	• Change string brand or increase string gauge
18) String breaks at nut or string post	• Burr in nut slot or on string post	• Have nut or string post either filed or sanded
19) String windings crossing over saddle	• Bridge plate is worn	• Have bridge plate overlayed with small piece of wood or have bridge plate replaced
	• Bridge and saddle are cut down too low, exposing too much string windings	• Check if shallow neck angle and low bridge are the reasons

20) String won't tune up smoothly. String jumps past desired pitch with a pinging sound	• String is binding in nut slot	• Have nut slots recut or re-angled
21) Lifting bridge	• Excessive dryness is shrinking top or excessive humidity is rejecting bridge	• Reglue bridge and maintain proper humidity levels (see Humidty section)
	• Inadequate amount of original glue at assembly	• Reglue bridge
	• Bridge glued directly to finish instead of bare wood or too much finish left at the perimeter, causing incomplete adhering	
	• Top too fragile to support chosen string gauge	• Decrease string gauge
	• Bridge-plate worn, causing string ball ends to break through to the top and directly pull up on bridge	• Replace bridge-plate or add small bridge-plate overlay and reglue bridge

			Have top examined by a luthier to determine which corrective action to take
22) Hump behind bridge. Bridge is still attached but angled up at its back side and diving down at the front side	• One, some, or all of these conditions exist:		
		• Excess humidity/Too little humidity	
		• Strings too heavy	
		• X-braces loose	
		• Bridge plate coming off or cracked at pin holes	
		• Saddle and bridge too high from steep neck angle	
23) Fretboard binding cracking or becoming unglued at fret ends	• Fretboard shrinkage causing frets to protrude and push on binding		• Replace missing or cracked binding or re-glue after trimming protruding fret ends

GLOSSARY

Action: the height of the strings above the fingerboard as determined by the adjustments to the saddle truss rod and nut.

Back: the back of the guitar body.

Back Brace: the braces glued to the back. They vary in number and their function is to maintain a structural arch and solidify the reflective capacity of the back.

Backlash: the amount of slack in the cog-to-worm-gear meshing in a guitar tuning machine.

Binding: a wood or plastic strip that binds the guitar top and/or back. It protects the softer guitar edges.

Bout: (see Upper or Lower Bout)

Bridge: the wooden platform that holds the strings and saddle.

Bridge Pin: the plastic, wood, or bone pin that holds the guitar string against the bridge plate.

Bridge Plate: the thin hardwood piece that fits between the X-brace. It governs the upward string pull and supports the string's ball end against pulling through the top.

Bridge Plate Overlay: a small, thin piece of hardwood overlayed on the existing bridgeplate to provide a new bearing surface for the crushing effect of the string's ball end.

Compensation: the amount of saddle adjustment needed to compensate for the string height, scale length, string composition, and gauge.

Compensated Saddle: after the compensation is factored, a compensated or intonationally adjusted saddle is sometimes required.

Dovetail Joint: the hidden neck joint on most acoustic guitars. The neck is glued and wedged into a wooden neck block. The flared V-shape is reminiscent of a dove's tail.

End Pin: the plastic or wood pin that is usually taper-fitted through the end block. It fastens a guitar strap to the body.

Feeler Gauge: a mechanics tool that measures tolerances in auto mobile repair. It is useful for measuring guitar tolerances at the nut.

Frets (Fretwire): the nickel or German silver T-shaped metal bars that are part of the fretboard. They are strategically spaced to provide proper intonation throughout the length of the fretboard.

Fretboard: the rosewood, ebony or plastic composite piece glued to the neck that holds the fretwire.

Fretboard Extension: the part of the fretboard that extends over the top of the guitar.

Fret Leveling: the process of trueing all frets to one another to create a level fretboard that contributes to a full setup.

Gear Ratio: the amount of full turns on a tuning machine that is required to make on complete revolution of the tuning post. Ratios range from 12:1 (finest) to 20:1 (most/finest).

Growth Rings: the wooden grain lines that are visible across a spruce or cedar top.

Headstock: the part of the guitar where the tuning gears are attached.

Heat Warping: a technique to force a neck into straightness by softening the glue joint between fretboard and neck. A heat bar controlled with time and temperature is typically used.

Hygrometer: a digital or analog gauge that measures relative humidity.

Intonation: the quality of an instrument being in tune across the entire fretboard.

Lacquer: the synthetic coating usually sprayed in multiple layers on wooden musical instruments to protect the wood from deteriorating from wear.

Lower Bout: the part of the guitar at its widest point across the face or back.

Luthier: originally french for "lute maker." Now it is used across the string instrument world to define a crafts person involved in making or repairing stringed musical instruments.

Lutherie: originally a french term for the "place where a lute is made." Now it refers to a shop that makes or repairs string instruments.

Machine Heads: the sealed tuning gears of a guitar.

Machine Screw Down Bushing: the screw down collar that hold the tuning machine tight against the headstock face.

Neck: the long wooden piece that the fretboard is attached to.

Neck Angle: the angle at which the neck is set to the body. It determines the height of the strings above the fretboard.

Neck Block: the mahogany block that is glued or bolted to the neck and visible through most soundholes.

Neck Heel: the part of the neck that extends down along the sides and ends at the back.

Neck Reset: removing of the neck and re-angling its relationship to the body to create a more playable string height.

Nut: the bone, wooden, or plastic piece at the beginning of the fretboard that separates the strings and is adjusted for playability at the first fret.

Nut Adjustment: filing the nut's string slots with an appropriate file or shimming from beneath are typical nut adjustment techniques.

Open-Geared Tuner: sometimes called a "vintage-style tuner", this is a tuner or tuning machine in which the gears are exposed rather than covered or sealed. High-end open-back tuners are preferred on smaller or lighter built guitars because they weigh less, which affects neck balance, and are, esthetically matched to a vintage appearance.

Peg Head: (see headstock)

Pickguard: a plastic or wood piece glued or raised to the guitar top finish to protect it from scratches.

Press Fit Bushing: open-geared machine-type tuners have a bushing that is press fit, not screwed down, to secure the tuner to the headstock.

Purfling: the wood or plastic decorative strip glued between the wood of the top, side, and back and the plastic or wood binding along the edge of the guitar.

Quarter Sawn: the technique of sawing wood appropriate for guitar-building to enhance strength and rigidity.

Saddle: the bone or plastic piece inserted into the bridge that suspends the guitar strings.

Scale Length: the distance between the nut and saddle.

Sealed Gear Machine: sealed-back, permanently lubricated tuning machines.

Setup: the adjustments to the truss rod, nut and saddle necessary for good playability and intonation. It can also include fret-leveling.

Side (or Rib): the curved parts of the guitar that rest on one's lap and under the strumming arm.

Soundhole: the (usually) round hole in the guitar top.

Soundhole Rosette: the decorative inlay surrounding the soundhole of the top.

Sound Port: a small hole situated at the side upper bout to help direct the volume toward the player.

Strap Button: the metal or plastic piece that is screwed into the neck heel and screwed or taper-fit into the heel block.

String Gauge: strings come in different thicknesses or gauges. They are commonly packaged in extra light, light, and medium gauges.

String Height: the height of the strings above the fretboard that is measured from the top of the 12th fret to the bottom of the string.

Tailblock (or End Block): the hidden mahogany block that secures the top and back to the sides and is located at the very bottom of the guitar, where the strap button sits.

Tone Bar: top braces other than the X-brace that contribute to the guitar's tone and structure.

Truss Rod: a metal, wood, or graphite neck reinforcement bar that stabilizes neck-bow. It may or may not be adjustable. The adjustment nut is located either at the headstock or under the soundhole.

Tuning Machines: the metal tuning gears located at the headstock are referred to as "tuning machines," "tuning gears," or "machine heads."

Upper Bout: the narrowest point across the face or back of the guitar.

X-brace: two internal braces running diagonally across the entire length of the guitar top and haped in an "X" that serve as structural support and help tonal clarity.

ORE GREAT GUITAR READS

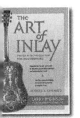

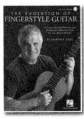

E ART OF INLAY – VISED & EXPANDED EDITION
sign & Technique for Fine odworking
Larry Robinson • Backbeat Books
31289.. $29.99
9780879308353

ECTRIC GUITAR DESIGN & VENTION
e Groundbreaking Innovations That aped the Modern Instrument
Tony Bacon • Backbeat Books
51794.. $29.99
9781617136405

E EVOLUTION OF NGERSTYLE GUITAR
ssical Guitar History and Repertoire m the 16th to the 20th Century
Laurence Juber • Hal Leonard
283983 Book/Online Audio.............. $24.99
9781540036247

JITAR DREAMS
llected Interviews, Articles and otographs
Andy Volk • Centerstream Publications
31538 Hardcover $29.99
9781574242645

STORY OF THE MERICAN GUITAR
3 to the Present Day
Tony Bacon • Backbeat Books
333186.. $29.99
9781617130335

INVENTING THE AMERICAN GUITAR
The Pre-Civil War Innovations of C.F. Martin and His Contemporaries
edited by Robert Shaw & Peter Szego • Hal Leonard
00333271 Hardcover $50.00
9781458405760

108 ROCK STAR GUITARS
by Lisa S. Johnson • Hal Leonard
00127925.. $54.00
9781480391475

PICKUPS, WINDINGS & MAGNETS
...And the Guitar Became Electric
by Mario Milan • Centerstream Publications
00001026.. $29.99
9781574242096

STAR GUITARS
101 Guitars That Rocked the World
by Dave Hunter • Voyageur Press
00139165.. $19.99
9781574242096

365 GUITARS, AMPS & EFFECTS YOU MUST PLAY
The Most Sublime, Bizarre and Outrageous Gear Ever
by Dave Hunter • Voyageur Press
00121129.. $21.99
9780760343661

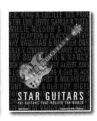